PLANT BASED DIET COOKBOOK

SNACK AND DESSERT RECIPES

Quick, Easy and Delicious Recipes
for a lifelong Health

Amanda Grant

Copyright © 2021 by Amanda Grant

Legal Disclaimer

The information contained in this book and its contents is not designed to replace any form of medical or professional advice; and is not meant to replace the need for independent medical, financial, legal, or other professional advice or service that may require. The content and information in this book have been provided for educational and entertainment purposes only.

The content and information contained in this book have been compiled from sources deemed reliable, and they are accurate to the best of the Author's knowledge, information and belief.

However, the Author cannot guarantee its accuracy and validity and therefore cannot be held liable for any errors and/or omissions.

Further, changes are periodically made to this book as needed. Where appropriate and/or necessary, you must consult a professional (including but not limited to your doctor, attorney, financial advisor, or other such professional) before using any of the suggested remedies, techniques, and/or information in this book.

Upon using this book's contents and information, you agree to hold harmless the Author from any damaged, costs and expenses, including any legal fees potentially resulting from the application of any of the information in this book. This disclaimer applies to any loss, damages, or injury caused by the use and application of this book's content, whether directly and indirectly, whether for breach of contract, tort, negligence, personal injury, criminal intent, or under any other circumstances.

You agree to accept all risks of using the information presented in this book. You agree that by continuing to read this book, where appropriate and/or necessary, you shall consult a professional (including but not limited to your doctor, attorney, financial advisor, or other such professional) before remedies, techniques, and/or information in this book.

TABLE OF CONTENTS

Snack & Dessert Recipes

Last-minute Macaroons

Servings: 10

Cooking Time: 15 Minutes

Ingredients:

- ➢ 3 cups coconut flakes, sweetened
- ➢ 9 ounces canned coconut milk, sweetened
- ➢ 1 teaspoon ground anise
- ➢ 1 teaspoon vanilla extract

Directions:

- ➢ Begin by preheating your oven to 325 degrees F. Line the cookie sheets with parchment paper.
- ➢ Thoroughly combine all the ingredients until everything is well incorporated.
- ➢ Use a cookie scoop to drop mounds of the batter onto the prepared cookie sheets.
- ➢ Bake for about 11 minutes until they are lightly browned. Bon appétit!

Nutrition Info: Per Serving: Calories: 125; Fat: 7.2g; Carbs: 14.3g; Protein: 1.1g

Apple & Cashew Quiche

Servings: 6

Cooking Time: 55 Minutes

Ingredients:

- ➢ 5 apples, peeled and cut into slices
- ➢ ½ cup pure maple syrup
- ➢ 1 tbsp fresh orange juice
- ➢ 1 tsp ground cinnamon
- ➢ ½ cup whole-grain flour
- ➢ ½ cup old-fashioned oats
- ➢ ½ cup finely chopped cashew
    - ➢ ⅔ cup pure date sugar
- ➢ ½ cup plant butter, softened

Directions:

- ➢ Preheat oven to 360 F. Place apples in a greased baking pan. Stir in maple syrup and orange juice. Sprinkle with ½ tsp of cinnamon. In a bowl, combine the flour, oats, cashew, sugar, and remaining cinnamon. Blend in the butter until the mixture crumbs. Pour over the apples and bake for 45 minutes.

Minty Fruit Salad

Servings: 4

Cooking Time: 5 Minutes

Ingredients:

- ¼ cup lemon juice (about 2 small lemons)
- 4teaspoons maple syrup or agave syrup
- 2 cups chopped pineapple
- 2 cups chopped strawberries
- 2 cups raspberries
- 1 cup blueberries
- 8 fresh mint leaves

Directions:

- Preparing the Ingredients
- Beginning with 1 mason jar, add the ingredients in this order:
- 1 tablespoon of lemon juice, 1 teaspoon of maple syrup, ½ cup of pineapple, ½ cup of strawberries, ½ cup of raspberries, ¼ cup of blueberries, and 2 mint leaves.
- Finish and Serve
- Repeat to fill 3 more jars. Close the jars tightly with lids.

➢ Place the airtight jars in the refrigerator for up to 3 days.

Nutrition Info: Per Serving: Calories: 138; Fat: 1g; Protein: 2g; Carbohydrates: 34g; Fiber: 8g; Sugar: 22g; Sodium: 6mg

Holiday Pecan Tart

Servings: 4

Cooking Time: 50 Minutes

Ingredients:

- ➤ 4 tbsp flax seed powder
- ➤ 1/3 cup whole-wheat flour
- ➤ ½ tsp salt
- ➤ ¼ cup cold plant butter, crumbled
- ➤ 3 tbsp pure malt syrup
- ➤ 3 tbsp flax seed powder + 9 tbsp water
- ➤ 2 cups toasted pecans, chopped
- ➤ 1 cup light corn syrup
- ➤ ½ cup pure date sugar
- ➤ 1 tbsp pure pomegranate molasses
- ➤ 4 tbsp plant butter, melted
- ➤ ½ tsp salt
- ➤ 2 tsp vanilla extract

Directions:

- ➤ Preheat the oven to 350 F. In a bowl, mix the flax seed powder with tbsp water and allow thickening for 5 minutes. Do this for the filling's flax egg too in a separate bowl. In a large bowl, combine flour and salt. Add in plant butter and whisk until crumbly. Pour in the crust's flax egg and maple syrup and mix until smooth dough forms. Flatten the dough on a flat surface, cover with plastic wrap, and refrigerate for 1 hour. Dust a working surface with flour, remove the dough onto the surface, and using a rolling pin, flatten the dough into a 1-inch diameter circle. Lay the dough on a greased pie pan and press to fit the shape of the pan. Trim the edges of the pan. Lay a parchment paper on the dough, pour on some baking beans and bake for 20 minutes. Remove the pan, pour out the baking beans, and allow cooling.

➢ In a bowl, mix the filling's flax egg, pecans, corn syrup, date sugar, pomegranate molasses, plant butter, salt, and vanilla. Pour and spread the mixture on the piecrust. Bake further for minutes or until the filling sets. Remove from the oven, decorate with more pecans, slice, and cool. Slice and serve.

Nutrition Info: Per Serving: Calories: 415; Fat: 25g; Protein: 7g; Carbohydrates: 41g; Fiber: 8g; Sugar: 22g; Sodium: 6mg

Pressure Cooker Apple Cupcakes

Servings: 4

Cooking Time: 25 Minutes

Ingredients:

- ➢ 1 cup canned applesauce
- ➢ 1 cup non-dairy milk
- ➢ 6 tbsp maple syrup + for sprinkling
- ➢ ¼ cup spelt flour
- ➢ ½ tsp apple pie spice
- ➢ A pinch of salt

Directions:

- ➢ In a bowl, combine the applesauce, milk, maple syrup, flour, apple pie spice, and salt. Scoop into 4 heat-proof ramekins. Drizzle with more syrup.
- ➢ Pour 1 cup of water in the IP and fit in a trivet. Place the ramekins on the trivet. Lock lid in place; set the time to 6 minutes on High. Once ready, perform a quick pressure release. Unlock the lid and let cool for a few minutes take out the ramekins. Allow to cool for 10 minutes and serve.

Nutrition Info: Per Serving: Calories: 163; Fat: 7.9g; Protein: 7g; Carbohydrates: 22g; Fiber: 1g; Sugar: 1g; Sodium: 174mg

Chocolate Mousse

Servings: 2

Cooking Time: 0 Minute

Ingredients:

- ➤ 6 drops liquid stevia extract
- ➤ ½ t. cinnamon
- ➤ 3 tbsp. cocoa powder, unsweetened
- ➤ 1 c. coconut milk

Directions:

- ➤ On the day before, place the coconut milk into the refrigerator overnight.
- ➤ Remove the coconut milk from the refrigerator; it should be very thick.
- ➤ Whisk in cocoa powder with an electric mixer.
- ➤ Add stevia and cinnamon and whip until combined.
- ➤ Place in individual bowls and serve and enjoy.

Nutrition Info: Per Serving: Calories: 288; Fat: 21g; Protein: 4g; Carbohydrates: 22g; Fiber: 1g; Sugar: 1g; Sodium: 95mg

Almond-date Energy Bites

Servings: 24

Cooking Time: 15 Minutes

Ingredients:

- ➢ 1 cup dates, pitted
- ➢ 1 cup unsweetened shredded coconut
- ➢ ¼ cup chia seeds
- ➢ ¾ cup ground almonds
- ➢ ¼ cup cocoa nibs, or non-dairy chocolate chips

Directions:

- ➢ Preparing the Ingredients.
- ➢ Purée everything in a food processor until crumbly and sticking together, pushing down the sides whenever necessary to keep it blending. If you don't have a food processor, you can mash soft Medjool dates. But if you're using harder baking dates, you'll have to soak them, then try to purée them in a blender.
- ➢ Finish and Serve
- ➢ Form the mix into 2balls and place them on a baking sheet lined with parchment or waxed paper. Put in the fridge to set for about 15 minutes. Use the softest dates you can find.

Medjool dates are the best for this purpose. The hard dates you see in the baking aisle of your supermarket are going to take a long time to blend up. If you use those, try soaking them in water for at least an hour before you start, and then start draining.

Nutrition Info: Per Serving: (1 bite) Calories 152; Total fat: 11g; Carbs: 13g; Fiber: 5g; Protein: 3g

Peach-mango Crumble (pressure Cooker)

Servings: 4-6

Cooking Time: 21 Minutes

Ingredients:

- ➢ 3 cups chopped fresh or frozen peaches
- ➢ 3 cups chopped fresh or frozen mangos
- ➢ 4 tablespoons unrefined sugar or pure maple syrup, divided
- ➢ 1 cup gluten-free rolled oats
- ➢ ½ cup shredded coconut, sweetened or unsweetened
- ➢ 2 tablespoons coconut oil or vegan margarine

Directions:

- ➢ Preparing the Ingredients. In a 6- to 7-inch round baking dish, toss together the peaches, mangos, and 2 tablespoons of sugar. In a food processor, combine the oats, coconut, coconut oil, and remaining 2 tablespoons of sugar. Pulse until combined. (If you use maple syrup, you'll need less coconut oil. Start with just the syrup and add oil if the mixture isn't sticking together.) Sprinkle the oat mixture over the fruit mixture.

➢ Cover the dish with aluminum foil. Put a trivet in the bottom of your electric pressure cooker's cooking pot and pour in a cup or two of water. Using a foil sling or silicone helper handles, lower the pan onto the trivet.

➢ High pressure for 6 minutes. Close and lock the lid, and select High Pressure for 6 minutes.

➢ Pressure Release. Once the cook time is complete, quick release the pressure. Unlock and remove the lid.

➢ Let cool for a few minutes before carefully lifting out the dish with oven mitts or tongs. Scoop out portions to serve.

Nutrition Info: Per Serving: Calories: 321; Total fat: 18g; Protein: 4g; Sodium: 2mg; Fiber: 7g

Lime Avocado Ice Cream

Servings: 4

Cooking Time: 10 Minutes

Ingredients:

- ➢ 2 large avocados, pitted
- ➢ Juice and zest of 3 limes
- ➢ 1/3 cup erythritol
- ➢ 1 ¾ cups coconut cream
- ➢ ¼ tsp vanilla extract

Directions:

- ➢ In a blender, combine the avocado pulp, lime juice and zest, erythritol, coconut cream, and vanilla extract. Process until the mixture is smooth. Pour the mixture into your ice cream maker and freeze based on the manufacturer's instructions. When ready, remove and scoop the ice cream into bowls. Serve immediately.

Nutrition Info: Per Serving: Calories: 122; Fat: 11g; Protein: 2,2g; Carbohydrates: 7,2g; Fiber: 3,8g; Sugar: 1g; Sodium: 9,6mg

Walnut Chocolate Squares

Servings: 6

Cooking Time: 10 Minutes

Ingredients:

- ➤ 3½ oz dairy-free dark chocolate
- ➤ 4 tbsp plant butter
- ➤ 1 pinch salt, ¼ cup walnut butter
- ➤ ½ tsp vanilla extract
- ➤ ¼ cup chopped walnuts to garnish

Directions:

- ➤ Pour the chocolate and plant butter in a safe microwave bowl and melt in the microwave for about to 2 minutes. Remove the bowl from the microwave and mix in the salt, walnut butter, and vanilla. Grease a small baking sheet with cooking spray and line with parchment paper. Pour in the batter and use a spatula to spread out into a 4 x 6-inch rectangle. Top with the chopped walnuts and chill in the refrigerator. Once set, cut into 1 x 1-inch squares. Serve while firming.

Nutrition Info: Per Serving: Calories: 163; Fat: 7.9g; Protein: 7g; Carbohydrates: 22g; Fiber: 1g; Sugar: 1g; Sodium: 174mg

Vegetable Mushroom Side Dish

Servings: 4

Cooking Time: 60 Minutes

Ingredients:

- ➤ 2 tbsp plant butter
- ➤ 1 large onion, diced
- ➤ 1 cup celery, diced
- ➤ ½ cup carrots, diced
- ➤ ½ tsp dried marjoram
- ➤ 1 tsp dried basil
- ➤ 2 cups chopped cremini mushrooms
- ➤ 1 cup vegetable broth
- ➤ ¼ cup chopped fresh parsley
- ➤ 1 medium whole-grain bread loaf, cubed

Directions:

- ➤ Melt the butter in large skillet and sauté the onion, celery, mushrooms, and carrots until softened, 5 minutes.
- ➤ Mix in the marjoram, basil, and season with salt and black pepper.
- ➤ Pour in the vegetable broth and mix in the parsley and bread. Cook until the broth reduces by half, 10 minutes.

➢ Pour the mixture into a baking dish and cover with foil. Bake in the oven at 375 F for 30 minutes.

➢ Uncover and bake further for 30 minutes or until golden brown on top and the liquid absorbs.

➢ Remove the dish from the oven and serve the stuffing.

Nutrition Info: Per Serving: Calories: 34; Fat: 1.5g; Protein: 3.5g; Carbohydrates: 3.6g; Fiber: 1.4g; Sugar: 2.1g; Sodium: 164mg

Chocolate Macaroons

Servings: 8

Cooking Time: 15 Minutes

Ingredients:

- ➢ 1 cup unsweetened shredded coconut
- ➢ 2 tablespoons cocoa powder
    - ➢ ⅔ cup coconut milk
- ➢ ¼ cup agave
- ➢ pinch of sea salt

Directions:

- ➢ Preparing the Ingredients.
- ➢ Preheat the oven to 350°F. Line a baking sheet with parchment paper. In a medium saucepan, cook all the ingredients over medium-high heat until a firm dough is formed. Scoop the dough into balls and place on the baking sheet.
- ➢ Bake for 15 minutes, remove from the oven, and let it cool on the baking sheet. Serve cooled macaroons.

Nutrition Info: Per Serving: Calories: 70; Fat: 4.9g; Protein: 1g; Carbohydrates: 7.6g; Fiber: 0.5; Sugar: 6.6g; Sodium: 16.3mg

Mixed Berry Yogurt Ice Pops

Servings: 6

Cooking Time: 5 Minutes

Ingredients:

- ➢ 2/3 cup avocado, halved and pitted
- ➢ 2/3 cup frozen berries, thawed
- ➢ 1 cup dairy-free yogurt
- ➢ ½ cup coconut cream
- ➢ 1 tsp vanilla extract

Directions:

- ➢ Pour the avocado pulp, berries, dairy-free yogurt, coconut cream, and vanilla extract. Process until smooth. Pour into ice pop sleeves and freeze for 8 or more hours. Enjoy the ice pops when ready.

Nutrition Info: Per Serving: Calories: 76; Fat: 3.9g; Protein: 2g; Carbohydrates: 11g; Fiber: 1g; Sugar: 9g; Sodium: 9mg

Risotto Bites

Servings: 12

Cooking Time: 20 Minutes

Ingredients:

- ½ cup panko bread crumbs
- 1 teaspoon paprika
- 1 teaspoon chipotle powder or ground cayenne pepper
- 1½ cups cold Green Pea Risotto
- Nonstick cooking spray

Directions:

- Preparing the Ingredients.
- Preheat the oven to 4ºF.
- Line a baking sheet with parchment paper.
- On a large plate, combine the panko, paprika, and chipotle powder. Set aside.
- Roll 2 tablespoons of the risotto into a ball.
- Gently roll in the bread crumbs, and place on the prepared baking sheet. Repeat to make a total of 12 balls.
- Spritz the tops of the risotto bites with nonstick cooking spray and bake for 15 to 20 minutes, until they begin to brown. Cool completely before

storing in a large airtight container in a single layer (add a piece of parchment paper for a second layer) or in a plastic freezer bag.

Nutrition Info: Calories: 100; Fat: 2g; Protein: 6g; Carbohydrates: 17g; Fiber: 5g; Sugar: 2g; Sodium: 165 mg

Brownie Bites

Servings: 8

Cooking Time: 0 Minutes

Ingredients:

- ¾ cup blanched almond flour
- ¾ cup cacao powder
- 2 tablespoons ground flaxseed
- ½ cup unsweetened vegan mini chocolate chips
- ¾ cup creamy almond butter, melted
- ¼ cup pure maple syrup
- 1 teaspoon pure vanilla extract

Directions:

- In a large bowl, mix together the almond flour, cocoa powder, flaxseed, and chocolate chips.
- Add the almond butter, maple syrup, and vanilla extract, and gently stir to combine.
- Using a sturdy spatula, stir and fold together until well incorporated.
- With your hands, make equal-sized balls from mixture.
- Arrange the balls onto a parchment paper-lined baking sheet in a single layer.

➢ Refrigerate to set for about 15 minutes before serving.

Nutrition Info: Per Serving: Calories: 290; Fat: 15g; Protein: 2g; Carbohydrates: 35g; Fiber: 2g; Sugar: 9g; Sodium: 9mg

Fudge

Servings: 18

Cooking Time: 5 Minutes

Ingredients:

➢ 1 cup vegan chocolate chips

➢ ½ cup soy milk

Directions:

➢ Line an 8-inch portion skillet with wax paper. Set aside. Clear some space in your refrigerator for this dish as you will need it later.

➢ Melt chocolate chips in a double boiler or add chocolate and almond spread to a medium, microwave-safe bowl. Melt it in the microwave in - second increments until chocolate melts. In between each 20-second burst, stir the chocolate until it is smooth.

➢ Empty the melted chocolate mixture into the lined skillet. Tap the sides of the skillet to make sure the mixture spreads into an even layer. Alternatively, use a spoon to make swirls on top.

➢ Move skillet to the refrigerator until it is firm. Remove the skillet from the refrigerator and cut fudge into 18 squares.

Sesame

Servings: 3

Cooking Time: 12 Minutes

Ingredients:

- ¾ cup vegan margarine, softened
- ½ cup light brown sugar
- 1 teaspoon pure vanilla extract
- 2 tablespoons pure maple syrup
- ¼ teaspoon salt
- 2 cups whole-grain flour
- ¾ cup sesame seeds, lightly toasted

Directions:

- Preparing the Ingredients
- In a large bowl, cream together the margarine and sugar until light and fluffy. Blend in the vanilla, maple syrup, and salt. Stir in the flour and sesame seeds and mix well.
- Roll the dough into a cylinder about 2 inches in diameter. Wrap it in plastic wrap and refrigerate for 1 hour or longer. Preheat the oven to 5°F.
- Slice the cookie dough into 1/8-inch-thick rounds and arrange on an ungreased baking sheet about 2 inches apart.

➢ Bake until light brown for about 12 minutes. When completely cool, store in an airtight container.

Nutrition Info: Per Serving: Calories: 90; Fat: 3.5g; Protein: 0.5g; Carbohydrates: 14.3g; Fiber: 0.3g; Sugar: 12.8g; Sodium: 17mg

Tacos

Servings: 4

Cooking Time: 30 Minutes

Ingredients:

- 6 Taco Shells
- For the slaw:
- 1 cup Red Cabbage, shredded
- 3 Scallions, chopped
- 1 cup Green Cabbage, shredded
- 1 cup Carrots, sliced
- For the dressing:
- 1 tbsp. Sriracha
- ¼ cup Apple Cider Vinegar
- ¼ tsp. Salt
- 2 tbsp. Sesame Oil
- 1 tbsp. Dijon Mustard
- 1 tbsp. Lime Juice
- ½ tbsp. Tamari
- 1 tbsp. Maple Syrup
- ¼ tsp. Salt

Directions:

- To start with, make the dressing, whisk all the ingredients in a small bowl until mixed well.

➤ Next, combine the slaw ingredients in another bowl and toss well.

➤ Finally, take a taco shell and place the slaw in it.

➤ Serve and enjoy.

Nutrition Info: Per Serving: Calories: 171; Fat: 21g; Protein: 15g; Carbohydrates: 33g; Fiber: 6g; Sugar: 1.8g; Sodium: 678mg

Kale Chips 2

Servings: 10

Cooking Time: 1 Hour 30 Minutes

Ingredients:

- ➢ ½ tsp. Smoked Paprika
- ➢ 2 bunches of Curly Kale
- ➢ 1 tsp. Garlic Powder
- ➢ ½ cup Nutritional Yeast
- ➢ 2 cups Cashew, soaked for 2 hours
- ➢ 1 tsp. Salt
- ➢ ½ cup Nutritional Yeast

Directions:

- ➢ To make these tasty, healthy chips place the kale in a large mixing bowl.
- ➢ Now, combine all the remaining ingredients in the high-speed blender and blend for 1 minute or until smooth.
- ➢ Next, pour this dressing over the kale chips and mix well with your hands.
- ➢ Then, preheat your oven to 225 ° F or 107 °C.
- ➢ Once heated, arrange the kale leaves on a large baking sheet leaving ample space between them.

➢ Bake the leaves for 80 to 90 minutes flipping them once in between.

➢ Finally, allow them to cool completely and then store them in an air-tight container.

Nutrition Info: Per Serving: Calories: 66; Fat: 3.9g; Protein: 2.5g; Carbohydrates: 7.3g; Fiber: 2.6g; Sugar: 1.8g; Sodium: 14mg

Green Salsa

Servings: 4

Cooking Time: 15 Minutes

Ingredients:

- ➢ 3 large heirloom tomatoes, chopped
- ➢ 1 green onion, finely chopped
- ➢ ½ bunch parsley, chopped
- ➢ 2 garlic cloves, minced
- ➢ 1 Jalapeño pepper, minced
- ➢ Juice of 1 lime
- ➢ ¼ cup olive oil Salt to taste
- ➢ Whole-grain tortilla chips

Directions:

- ➢ Combine the tomatoes, green onion, parsley, garlic, jalapeño pepper, lime juice, olive oil, and salt in a bowl. Let it rest for minutes at room temperature. Serve with tortilla chips.

Nutrition Info: Per Serving: Calories: 90; Fat: 3.5g; Protein: 0.5g; Carbohydrates: 14.3g; Fiber: 0.3g; Sugar: 12.8g; Sodium: 17mg

Kentucky Cauliflower With Mashed Parsnips

Servings: 6

Cooking Time: 35 Minutes

Ingredients:

- ½ cup unsweetened almond milk
- ¼ cup coconut flour
- ¼ tsp cayenne pepper
- ½ cup whole-grain breadcrumbs
- ½ cup grated plant-based mozzarella
- 30 oz cauliflower florets
- 1 lb parsnips, peeled and quartered
- 3 tbsp melted plant butter
- A pinch of nutmeg
- 1 tsp cumin powder
- 1 cup coconut cream
- 2 tbsp sesame oil

Directions:

- Preheat oven to 425 F and line a baking sheet with parchment paper.
- In a small bowl, combine almond milk, coconut flour, and cayenne pepper. In another bowl, mix salt, breadcrumbs, and plant-based mozzarella

cheese. Dip each cauliflower floret into the milk mixture, coating properly, and then into the cheese mixture. Place the breaded cauliflower on the baking sheet and bake in the oven for 30 minutes, turning once after 15 minutes.

➢ Make slightly salted water in a saucepan and add the parsnips. Bring to boil over medium heat for 15 minutes or until the parsnips are fork tender. Drain and transfer to a bowl. Add in melted plant butter, cumin powder, nutmeg, and coconut cream. Puree the ingredients using an immersion blender until smooth. Spoon the parsnip mash into serving plates and drizzle with some sesame oil. Serve with the baked cauliflower when ready.

Nutrition Info: Per Serving: Calories: 150; Fat: 8.5g; Protein: 7.5g; Carbohydrates: 45.3g; Fiber: 4.3g; Sugar: 6.8g; Sodium: 87mg

Pesto Zucchini Noodles

Servings: 4

Cooking Time: 0 Minutes

Ingredients:

- ➢ 4 little zucchini ends trimmed
- ➢ Cherry tomatoes
- ➢ 2 t. fresh lemon juice
- ➢ 1/3 c olive oil (best if extra-virgin)
- ➢ 2 cups packed basil leaves
- ➢ 2 c. garlic
- ➢ Salt and pepper to taste

Directions:

- ➢ Spiral zucchini into noodles and set to the side.
- ➢ In a food processor, combine the basil and garlic and chop. Slowly add olive oil while chopping. Then pulse blend it until thoroughly mixed.
- ➢ In a big bowl, place the noodles and pour pesto sauce over the top. Toss to combine.
- ➢ Garnish with tomatoes and serve and enjoy.

Nutrition Info: Per Serving: Calories: 225; Fat: 19.7g; Protein: 7.5g; Carbohydrates: 4.2g; Fiber: 4.3g; Sugar:1g; Sodium: 361mg

Mixed Vegetables With Basil

Servings: 4

Cooking Time: 40 Minutes

Ingredients:

- 2 medium zucchinis, chopped
- 2 medium yellow squash, chopped
- 1 red onion, cut into 1-inch wedges
- 1 red bell pepper, diced
- 1 cup cherry tomatoes, halved
- 4 tbsp olive oil
- Salt and black pepper to taste
- 3 garlic cloves, minced
- 2/3 cup whole-wheat breadcrumbs
- 1 lemon, zested
- ¼ cup chopped fresh basil

Directions:

- Preheat the oven to 450 F and lightly grease a large baking sheet with cooking spray.
- In a medium bowl, add the zucchini, yellow squash, red onion, bell pepper, tomatoes, olive oil, salt, black pepper, and garlic. Toss well and spread the mixture on the baking sheet. Roast in

the oven for to 30 minutes or until the vegetables are tender, while stirring every 5 minutes.

➢ Meanwhile, heat the olive oil in a medium skillet and sauté the garlic until fragrant. Mix in the breadcrumbs, lemon zest, and basil. Cook for 2 to minutes. Remove the vegetables from the oven and toss in the breadcrumb's mixture. Serve warm.

Nutrition Info: Per Serving: Calories: 120; Fat: 4-7g; Protein: 1.5g; Carbohydrates: 5g; Fiber: 4.3g; Sugar:1g; Sodium: 40mg

Za'atar Roasted Zucchini Sticks

Servings: 5

Cooking Time: 1 Hour 35 Minutes

Ingredients:

➢ 1 ½ pounds zucchini, cut into sticks lengthwise

➢ 2 garlic cloves, crushed

➢ 2 tablespoons extra-virgin olive oil

➢ 1 teaspoon za'atar spice

➢ Kosher salt and ground black pepper, to taste

Directions:

➢ Toss the zucchini with the remaining ingredients.

➢ Lay the zucchini sticks in a single layer on a parchment-lined baking pan.

➢ Bake at 2 degrees F for about 90 minutes until crisp and golden. Zucchini sticks will crisp up as they cool.

➢ Bon appétit!

Nutrition Info: Per Serving: Calories: 85; Fat: 6.1g; Carbs: 5.7g; Protein: 4.1g

Tangy Fruit Salad With Lemon Dressing

Servings: 4

Cooking Time: 15 Minutes

- ➤ 1/2 pound mixed berries
- ➤ 1/2 pound apples, cored and diced
- ➤ 8 ounces red grapes
- ➤ 2 kiwis, peeled and diced
- ➤ 2 large oranges, peeled and sliced
- ➤ 2 bananas, sliced
- ➤ Lemon Dressing:
- ➤ 2 tablespoons fresh lemon juice
- ➤ 1 teaspoon fresh ginger, peeled and minced
- ➤ 4 tablespoons agave syrup

Directions:

- ➤ Mix all the ingredients for the salad until well combined.
- ➤ Then, in a small mixing bowl, whisk all the lemon dressing ingredients.
- ➤ Dress your salad and serve well chilled. Bon appétit!

Nutrition Info: Per Serving: Calories: 223; Fat: 0.8g; Carbs: 56.1g; Protein: 2.4g

Nutty Date Cake

Servings: 4

Cooking Time: 1 Hour 30 Minutes

Ingredients:

- ½ cup cold plant butter, cut in pieces
- 1 tbsp flax seed powder
- ½ cup whole-wheat flour
- ¼ cup chopped pecans and walnuts
- 1 tsp baking powder
- 1 tsp baking soda
- 1 tsp cinnamon powder
- 1 tsp salt
- 1/3 cup pitted dates, chopped
- ½ cup pure date sugar
- 1 tsp vanilla extract
- ¼ cup pure date syrup for drizzling.

Directions:

- Preheat oven to 350 F and lightly grease a round baking dish with some plant butter. In a small bowl, mix the flax seed powder with 3 tbsp water and allow thickening for 5 minutes to make the flax egg.

➢ In a food processor, add the flour, nuts, baking powder, baking soda, cinnamon powder, and salt. Blend until well combined. Add 1/3 cup of water, dates, date sugar, and vanilla. Process until smooth with tiny pieces of dates evident.

➢ Pour the batter into the baking dish and bake in the oven for 1 hour and 10 minutes or until a toothpick inserted comes out clean. Remove the dish from the oven, invert the cake onto a serving platter to cool, drizzle with the date syrup, slice, and serve.

Nutrition Info: Per Serving: Calories: 444; Fat: 31.7g; Carbs: 41g; Protein: 8.4g

Tempting Quinoa Tabbouleh

Servings: 6

Cooking Time: 10 Minutes

Ingredients:

- ➢ 1 cup of well-rinsed quinoa
- ➢ 1 finely minced garlic clove
- ➢ ½ teaspoon of kosher salt
- ➢ ½ cup of extra virgin olive oil
- ➢ 2 tablespoons of fresh lemon juice
- ➢ Freshly ground black pepper
- ➢ 2 Persian cucumbers, cut into ¼-inch pieces
- ➢ 2 thinly sliced scallions
- ➢ 1 pint of halved cherry tomatoes
- ➢ ½ cup of chopped fresh mint
- ➢ 2/3 cup of chopped parsley

Directions:

- ➢ Put a medium saucepan on high heat and boil the quinoa mixed with salt in ¼ cups of water. Decrease the heat to medium-low, cover the pot, and simmer everything until the quinoa is tender. The entire process will take 10 minutes. Remove the quinoa from heat and allow it to stand for 5 minutes. Fluff it with a fork.

➢ In a small bowl, whisk the garlic with the lemon juice. Add the olive oil gradually. Mix the salt and pepper to taste.

➢ On a baking sheet, spread the quinoa and allow it to cool. Shift it to a large bowl and mix ¼ of the dressing.

➢ Add the tomatoes, scallions, herbs, and cucumber. Give them a good toss and season everything with pepper and salt. Add the remaining dressing.

Nutrition Info: Per Serving: Calories: 147; Fat: 5.7g; Carbs: 38.5g; Protein: 7.6g

Roasted Carrot And Bean Dip

Servings: 10

Cooking Time: 55 Minutes

Ingredients:

- 1 ½ pounds carrots, trimmed
- 2 tablespoons olive oil
- 4 tablespoons tahini
- 8 ounces canned cannellini beans, drained
- 1 teaspoon garlic, chopped
- 2 tablespoons lemon juice
- 2 tablespoons soy sauce
- Sea salt and ground black pepper, to taste
- 1/2 teaspoon paprika
- 1/2 teaspoon dried dill
- 1/4 cup pepitas, toasted

Directions:

- Begin by preheating your oven to 390 degrees F. Line a roasting pan with parchment paper.
- Now, toss the carrots with the olive oil and arrange them on the prepared roasting pan.
- Roast the carrots for about 50 minutes or until tender. Transfer the roasted carrots to the bowl of your food processor.

49

➢ Add in the tahini, beans, garlic, lemon juice, soy sauce, salt, black pepper, paprika and dill. Process until your dip is creamy and uniform.

➢ Garnish with toasted pepitas and serve with dippers of choice. Bon appétit!

Nutrition Info: Per Serving: Calories: 121; Fat: 8.3g; Carbs: 11.2g; Protein: 2.8g

Pepita Cheese Tomato Chips

Servings: 6

Cooking Time: 15 Minutes

Ingredients:

➢ 5 tomatoes, sliced

➢ ¼ cup olive oil

➢ ½ cup pepitas seeds

➢ 1 tbsp nutritional yeast

➢ Salt and black pepper, to taste

➢ 1 tsp garlic puree

Directions:

➢ Preheat oven to 400 F. Over the sliced tomatoes, drizzle olive oil. In a food processor, add pepitas seeds, nutritional yeast, garlic, salt, and pepper and pulse until the desired consistency is attained. Toss in tomato slices to coat. Set the tomato slices on a baking pan and bake for minutes.

Cinnamon Granola

Servings: 4

Cooking Time: 25 Minutes

Ingredients:

> ➢ 1 ½ t. cinnamon, ground
> ➢ 4 tbsp. maple syrup
> ➢ 1/5 oz. nuts
> ➢ 1 tbsp. chia seeds
> ➢ 5 tbsp. of the following:
> ➢ coconut flakes, unsweetened
> ➢ flaxseed meal

Directions:

> ➢ Bring the oven to 350 heat setting.
> ➢ In a medium mixing bowl, combine the flaxseed, coconut, chia seed, nuts, and maple syrup. Mix well until combined.
> ➢ Line a cookie sheet with parchment and spread the mixture in a single layer on the cookie sheet.
> ➢ Across the top, sprinkle the cinnamon.
> ➢ Place the cookie sheet in the oven, and wait for 20 minutes, approximately.
> ➢ Once done, take it out and allow the granola to cool while still on the sheet.

➢ Once cool, crumble to your desired liking and enjoy.

Nutrition Info: Per Serving: Calories: 118; Fat: 4.5g; Carbs: 19g; Protein: 2.5g

Old-fashioned Cookies

Servings: 12

Cooking Time: 45 Minutes

Ingredients:

- 1 cup all-purpose flour
- 1 teaspoon baking powder
- A pinch of salt
- A pinch of grated nutmeg
- 1/2 teaspoon ground cinnamon
- 1/4 teaspoon ground cardamom
- 1/2 cup peanut butter
- 2 tablespoons coconut oil, room temperature
- 2 tablespoons almond milk
- 1/2 cup brown sugar
- 1 teaspoon vanilla extract
- 1 cup vegan chocolate chips

Directions:

- In a mixing bowl, combine the flour, baking powder and spices.
- In another bowl, combine the peanut butter, coconut oil, almond milk, sugar and vanilla. Stir the wet mixture into the dry ingredients and stir until well combined.

➢ Fold in the chocolate chips. Place the batter in your refrigerator for about minutes. Shape the batter into small cookies and arrange them on a parchment-lined cookie pan.

➢ Bake in the preheated oven at 350 degrees F for approximately 11 minutes. Transfer them to a wire rack to cool slightly before serving. Bon appétit!

Nutrition Info: Per Serving: Calories: 167; Fat: 8.6g; Carbs: 19.6g; Protein: 2.7g

Chocolate Mint Grasshopper Pie

Servings: 4

Cooking Time: 0 Minute

Ingredients:

- ➢ For the Crust:
- ➢ 1 cup dates, soaked in warm water for 10 minutes in water, drained
- ➢ 1/8 teaspoons salt
- ➢ 1/2 cup pecans
- ➢ 1 teaspoons cinnamon
- ➢ 1/2 cup walnuts
- ➢ For the Filling:
- ➢ ½ cup mint leaves
- ➢ 2 cups of cashews, soaked in warm water for 10 minutes in water, drained
- ➢ 2 tablespoons coconut oil
- ➢ 1/4 cup and 2 tablespoons of agave
- ➢ 1/4 teaspoons spirulina
- ➢ 1/4 cup water

Directions:

- ➢ Prepare the crust, and for this, place all its ingredients in a food processor and pulse for 3 to 5 minutes until the thick paste comes together.

➢ Take a 6-inch springform pan, grease it with oil, place crust mixture in it and spread and press the mixture evenly in the bottom and along the sides, and freeze until required.

➢ Prepare the filling and for this, place all its ingredients in a food processor, and pulse for 2 minutes until smooth.

➢ Pour the filling into prepared pan, smooth the top, and freeze for hours until set.

➢ Cut pie into slices and then serve.

Nutrition Info: Calories: 223.7 Cal ;Fat: 7.5 g :Carbs: 36 g ;Protein: 2.5 g ;Fiber: 1 g

Waffles With Almond Flour

Servings: 4

Cooking Time: 15 Minutes

Ingredients:

- ➢ 1 cup almond milk
- ➢ 2 tbsps. chia seeds
- ➢ 2 tsp lemon juice
- ➢ 4 tbsps. coconut oil
- ➢ 1/2 cup almond flour
- ➢ 2 tbsps. maple syrup
- ➢ Cooking spray or cooking oil

Directions:

- ➢ Mix coconut milk with lemon juice in a mixing bowl.
- ➢ Leave it for 5-8 minutes on room temperature to turn it into butter milk.
- ➢ Once coconut milk is turned into butter milk, add chai seeds into milk and whisk together.
- ➢ Add other ingredients in milk mixture and mix well.
- ➢ Preheat a waffle iron and spray it with coconut oil spray.

➢ Pour 2 tbsp. of waffle mixture into the waffle machine and cook until golden.

➢ Top with some berries and serve hot.

➢ Enjoy with black coffee!

Nutrition Info: Protein: 5% 15 kcal Fat: 71% 199 kcal Carbohydrates: 23% 66 kcal

Cashew-chocolate Truffles

Servings: 12

Cooking Time: 0 Minutes

Ingredients:

- ➢ 1 cup raw cashews, soaked in water overnight
- ➢ ¾ cup pitted dates
- ➢ 2 tablespoons coconut oil
- ➢ 1 cup unsweetened shredded coconut, divided
- ➢ 1 to 2 tablespoons cocoa powder, to taste

Directions:

- ➢ Preparing the Ingredients.
- ➢ In a food processor, combine the cashews, dates, coconut oil, ½ cup of shredded coconut, and cocoa powder. Pulse until fully incorporated; it will resemble chunky cookie dough. Spread the remaining ½ cup of shredded coconut on a plate.
- ➢ Form the mixture into tablespoon-size balls and roll on the plate to cover with the shredded coconut. Transfer to a parchment paper–lined plate or baking sheet. Repeat to make 12 truffles.
- ➢ Finish and Serve

➢ Place the truffles in the refrigerator for 1 hour to set. Transfer the truffles to a storage container or freezer-safe bag and seal.

Nutrition Info: Per Serving: (1 truffle) Calories 238: Fat: 18g; Protein: 3g; Carbohydrates: 16g; Fiber: 4g; Sugar: 9g; Sodium: 9mg

Country-style Apricot Dump Cake

Servings: 8

Cooking Time: 10 Minutes

Ingredients:

- ➤ 10 apricots, pitted and halved
- ➤ 1 tablespoon crystallized ginger
- ➤ 1/4 cup brown sugar
- ➤ 1 cup all-purpose flour
- ➤ 1 teaspoon baking powder
- ➤ 1/2 teaspoon ground cinnamon
- ➤ 4 tablespoons agave syrup
- ➤ A pinch of kosher salt
- ➤ A pinch of grated nutmeg
- ➤ 1/4 cup coconut oil, room temperature
- ➤ 1/2 cup almond milk

Directions:

- ➤ Arrange the apricots on the bottom of a lightly oiled baking pan. Sprinkle ginger and brown sugar over them.
- ➤ In a mixing bowl, thoroughly combine the flour, baking powder, cinnamon, agave syrup, salt and nutmeg.

➤ Add in the coconut oil and almond milk and mix until everything is well incorporated. Spread the topping mixture over the fruit layer.

➤ Bake your cake at 360 degrees F for about minutes or until the top is golden brown. Bon appétit!

Nutrition Info: Per Serving: Calories: 226; Fat: 7.5g; Carbs: 38.8g; Protein: 2.4g

Chocolate Cookies

Servings: 4

Cooking Time: 5 Minutes

Ingredients:

- ➤ 1/2 cup coconut oil
- ➤ 1 cup agave syrup
- ➤ 1/2 cup cocoa powder
- ➤ 1/2 teaspoon salt, 2 cups peanuts, chopped
- ➤ 1 cup peanut butter
- ➤ 2 cups sunflower seeds

Directions:

- ➤ Take a small saucepan, place it over medium heat, add the first three ingredients, and cook for 3 minutes until melted.
- ➤ Boil the mixture for 1 minute, then remove the pan from heat and stir in salt and butter until smooth.
- ➤ Fold in nuts and seeds until combined, then drop the mixture in the form of molds onto the baking sheet lined with wax paper and refrigerate for minutes.

Nutrition Info: Calories: 148 Cal ;Fat: 7.4 g; Carbs: 20 g ;Protein: 1.5 g ;Fiber: 0.6 g

Mango Coconut Cheesecake

Servings: 4

Cooking Time: 0 Minute

Ingredients:

- ➢ For the Crust:
- ➢ 1 cup macadamia nuts
- ➢ 1 cup dates, pitted, soaked in hot water for 10 minutes
- ➢ For the Filling:
- ➢ 2 cups cashews, soaked in warm water for 10 minutes
- ➢ 1/2 cup and 1 tablespoon maple syrup
- ➢ 1/3 cup and 2 tablespoons coconut oil
- ➢ 1/4 cup lemon juice
- ➢ 1/2 cup and 2 tablespoons coconut milk, unsweetened, chilled
- ➢ For the Topping:
- ➢ 1 cup fresh mango slices

Directions:

- ➢ Prepare the crust, and for this, place nuts in a food processor and process until mixture resembles crumbs.

➤ Drain the dates, add them to the food processor and blend for minutes until thick mixture comes together.

➤ Take a 4-inch cheesecake pan, place date mixture in it, spread and press evenly, and set aside.

➤ Prepare the filling and for this, place all its ingredients in a food processor and blend for 3 minutes until smooth.

➤ Pour the filling into the crust, spread evenly, and then freeze for 4 hours until set.

➤ Top the cake with mango slices and then serve.

Nutrition Info: Calories: 200 Cal ;Fat: 11 g :Carbs: 22.5 g ;Protein: 2 g ;Fiber: 1 g

Stuffed Jalapeño Bites

Servings: 6

Cooking Time: 15 Minutes

Ingredients:

- ➢ 1/2 cup raw sunflower seeds, soaked overnight and drained
- ➢ 4 tablespoons scallions, chopped
- ➢ 1 teaspoon garlic, minced
- ➢ 3 tablespoons nutritional yeast
- ➢ 1/2 cup cream of onion soup
- ➢ 1/2 teaspoon cayenne pepper
- ➢ 1/2 teaspoon mustard seeds
- ➢ 12 jalapeños, halved and seeded
- ➢ 1/2 cup breadcrumbs

Directions:

- ➢ In your food processor or high-speed blender, blitz raw sunflower seeds, scallions, garlic, nutritional yeast, soup, cayenne pepper and mustard seeds until well combined.
- ➢ Spoon the mixture into the jalapeños and top them with the breadcrumbs.

➢ Bake in the preheated oven at 400 degrees F for about 1minutes or until the peppers have softened. Serve warm.

➢ Bon appétit!

Nutrition Info: Per Serving: Calories: 108; Fat: 6.6g; Carbs: 7.3g; Protein: 5.3g

Easy Lebanese Toum

Servings: 6

Cooking Time: 10 Minutes

Ingredients:

- ➢ 2 heads garlic
- ➢ 1 teaspoon coarse sea salt
- ➢ 1 ½ cups olive oil
- ➢ 1 lemon, freshly squeezed
- ➢ 2 cups carrots, cut into matchsticks

Directions:

- ➢ Puree the garlic cloves and salt in your food processor of a high-speed blender until creamy and smooth, scraping down the sides of the bowl.
- ➢ Gradually and slowly, add in the olive oil and lemon juice, alternating between these two ingredients to create a fluffy sauce.
- ➢ Blend until the sauce has thickened. Serve with carrot sticks and enjoy!

Nutrition Info: Per Serving: Calories: 252; Fat: 27g; Carbs: 3.1g; Protein: 0.4g

Peppery Hummus Dip

Servings: 10

Cooking Time: 10 Minutes

Ingredients:

- ➢ 20 ounces canned or boiled chickpeas, drained
- ➢ 1/4 cup tahini
- ➢ 2 garlic cloves, minced
- ➢ 2 tablespoons lemon juice, freshly squeezed
- ➢ 1/2 cup chickpea liquid
- ➢ 2 red roasted peppers, seeded and sliced
- ➢ 1/2 teaspoon paprika
- ➢ 1 teaspoon dried basil
- ➢ Sea salt and ground black pepper, to taste
- ➢ 2 tablespoons olive oil

Directions:

- ➢ Blitz all the ingredients, except for the oil, in your blender or food processor until your desired consistency is reached.
- ➢ Place in your refrigerator until ready to serve.
- ➢ Serve with toasted pita wedges or chips, if desired. Bon appétit!

Nutrition Info: Per Serving: Calories: 155; Fat: 7.9g; Carbs: 17.4g; Protein: 5.9g

Cherry Tomatoes With Hummus

Servings: 8

Cooking Time: 10 Minutes

Ingredients:

➢ 1/2 cup hummus, preferably homemade

➢ 2 tablespoons vegan mayonnaise

➢ 1/4 cup scallions, chopped

➢ 16 cherry tomatoes, scoop out pulp

➢ 2 tablespoons fresh cilantro, chopped

Directions:

➢ In a mixing bowl, thoroughly combine the hummus, mayonnaise and scallions.

➢ Divide the hummus mixture between the tomatoes. Garnish with fresh cilantro and serve.

➢ Bon appétit!

Nutrition Info: Per Serving: Calories: 49; Fat: 2.5g; Carbs: 4.7g; Protein: 1.3g

Berry Compote With Red Wine

Servings: 4

Cooking Time: 15 Minutes

Ingredients:

- ➤ 4 cups mixed berries, fresh or frozen
- ➤ 1 cup sweet red wine
- ➤ 1 cup agave syrup
- ➤ 1/2 teaspoon star anise
- ➤ 1 cinnamon stick
- ➤ 3-4 cloves
- ➤ A pinch of grated nutmeg
- ➤ A pinch of sea salt

Directions:

- ➤ Add all ingredients to a saucepan. Cover with water by inch. Bring to a boil and immediately reduce the heat to a simmer.
- ➤ Let it simmer for 9 to 11 minutes. Allow it to cool completely.
- ➤ Bon appétit!

Nutrition Info: Per Serving: Calories: 260; Fat: 0.5g; Carbs: 64.1g; Protein: 1.1g

Avocado With Tahini Sauce

Servings: 4

Cooking Time: 10 Minutes

Ingredients:

- ➢ 2 large-sized avocados, pitted and halved
- ➢ 4 tablespoons tahini
- ➢ 4 tablespoons soy sauce
- ➢ 1 tablespoon lemon juice
- ➢ 1/2 teaspoon red pepper flakes
- ➢ Sea salt and ground black pepper, to taste
- ➢ 1 teaspoon garlic powder

Directions:

- ➢ Place the avocado halves on a serving platter.
- ➢ Mix the tahini, soy sauce, lemon juice, red pepper, salt, black pepper and garlic powder in a small bowl. Divide the sauce between the avocado halves.
- ➢ Bon appétit!

Nutrition Info: Per Serving: Calories: 304; Fat: 25.7g; Carbs: 17.6g; Protein: 6g

Fruit And Almond Crisp

Servings: 8

Cooking Time: 45 Minutes

Ingredients:

- ➢ 4 cups peaches, pitted and sliced
- ➢ 3 cups plums, pitted and halved
- ➢ 1 tablespoon lemon juice, freshly squeezed
- ➢ 1 cup brown sugar
- ➢ For the topping:
- ➢ 2 cups rolled oats
- ➢ 1/2 cup oat flour
- ➢ 1 teaspoon baking powder
- ➢ 4 tablespoons water
- ➢ 1/2 cup almonds, slivered
- ➢ 1/2 teaspoon vanilla extract
- ➢ 1/2 teaspoon almond extract
- ➢ 1/4 teaspoon ground cloves
- ➢ 1/4 teaspoon ground cinnamon
- ➢ A pinch of kosher salt
- ➢ A pinch of grated nutmeg
- ➢ 5 ounces coconut oil, softened

Directions:

- ➢ Start by preheating your oven to 350 degrees F.

- ➢ Arrange the fruits on the bottom of a lightly oiled baking pan. Sprinkle lemon juice and 1/cup of brown sugar over them.
- ➢ In a mixing bowl, thoroughly combine the oats, oat flour, baking powder, water, almonds, vanilla, almond extract, ground cloves, cinnamon, salt, nutmeg and coconut oil.
- ➢ Spread the topping mixture over the fruit layer.
- ➢ Bake in the preheated oven for about 4minutes or until golden brown. Bon appétit!

Nutrition Info: Per Serving: Calories: 409; Fat: 19.1g; Carbs: 55.6g; Protein: 7.7g

Chocolate And Avocado Pudding

Servings: 1

Cooking Time: 0 Minute

Ingredients:

- ➢ 1 small avocado, pitted, peeled
- ➢ 1 small banana, mashed
- ➢ 1/3 cup cocoa powder, unsweetened
- ➢ 1 tablespoon cacao nibs, unsweetened
- ➢ 1/4 cup maple syrup
- ➢ 1/3 cup coconut cream

Directions:

- ➢ Add avocado in a food processor along with cream and then pulse for 2 minutes until smooth.
- ➢ Add remaining ingredients, blend until mixed, and then tip the pudding in a container.
- ➢ Cover the container with a plastic wrap; it should touch the pudding and refrigerate for hours.
- ➢ Serve straight away.

Nutrition Info: Calories: 87 Cal ;Fat: 7 g :Carbs: 9 g ;Protein: 1.5 g ;Fiber: 3.2 g

Brownie Energy Bites

Servings: 2

Cooking Time: 0 Minute

Ingredients:

➢ 1/2 cup walnuts

➢ 1 cup Medjool dates, chopped

➢ 1/2 cup almonds

➢ 1/8 teaspoon salt

➢ 1/2 cup shredded coconut flakes

➢ 1/3 cup and 2 teaspoons cocoa powder, unsweetened

Directions:

➢ Place almonds and walnuts in a food processor and pulse for 3 minutes until the dough starts to come together.

➢ Add remaining ingredients, reserving ¼ cup of coconut and pulse for minutes until incorporated.

➢ Shape the mixture into balls, roll them in remaining coconut until coated, and refrigerate for 1 hour.

➢ Serve straight away

Nutrition Info: Calories: 174.6 Cal ;Fat: 8.1 g :Carbs: 25.5 g ;Protein: 4.1 g ;Fiber: 4.4 g

Easy Mocha Fudge

Servings: 20

Cooking Time: 1 Hour 10 Minutes

Ingredients:

- ➢ 1 cup cookies, crushed
- ➢ 1/2 cup almond butter
- ➢ 1/4 cup agave nectar
- ➢ 6 ounces dark chocolate, broken into chunks
- ➢ 1 teaspoon instant coffee
- ➢ A pinch of grated nutmeg
- ➢ A pinch of salt

Directions:

- ➢ Line a large baking sheet with parchment paper.
- ➢ Melt the chocolate in your microwave and add in the remaining ingredients; stir to combine well.
- ➢ Scrape the batter into a parchment-lined baking sheet. Place it in your freezer for at least 1 hour to set.
- ➢ Cut into squares and serve. Bon appétit!

Nutrition Info: Per Serving: Calories: 105; Fat: 5.6g; Carbs: 12.9g; Protein: 1.1g

Strawberry Mousse

Servings: 4

Cooking Time: 15 Minutes

Ingredients:

➢ 8 ounces coconut milk, unsweetened

➢ 2 tablespoons honey

➢ 5 strawberries

Directions:

➢ Place berries in a blender and pulse until the smooth mixture comes together.

➢ Place milk in a bowl, whisk until whipped, and then add remaining ingredients and stir until combined.

➢ Refrigerate the mousse for 10 minutes and then serve.

Nutrition Info: Calories: 145 Cal ;Fat: 23 g :Carbs: 15 g ;Protein: 5 g ;Fiber: 1 g

Brownie Batter

Servings: 4

Cooking Time: 0 Minute

Ingredients:

- 4 Medjool dates, pitted, soaked in warm water
- 1.5 ounces chocolate, unsweetened, melted
- 2 tablespoons maple syrup
- 4 tablespoons tahini
- ½ teaspoon vanilla extract, unsweetened
- 1 tablespoon cocoa powder, unsweetened
- 1/8 teaspoon sea salt
- 1/8 teaspoon espresso powder
- 2 to 4 tablespoons almond milk, unsweetened

Directions:

- Place all the ingredients in a food processor and process for 2 minutes until combined.
- Set aside until required.

Nutrition Info: Calories: 44 Cal ;Fat: 1 g :Carbs: 6 g ;Protein: 2 g ;Fiber: 0 g

Spiced Roasted Cauliflower

Servings: 6

Cooking Time: 25 Minutes

Ingredients:

- ➢ 1 ½ pounds cauliflower florets
- ➢ 1/4 cup olive oil
- ➢ 4 tablespoons apple cider vinegar
- ➢ 2 cloves garlic, pressed
- ➢ 1 teaspoon dried basil
- ➢ 1 teaspoon dried oregano
- ➢ Sea salt and ground black pepper, to taste

Directions:

- ➢ Begin by preheating your oven to 420 degrees F.
- ➢ Toss the cauliflower florets with the remaining ingredients.
- ➢ Arrange the cauliflower florets on a parchment-lined baking sheet. Bake the cauliflower florets in the preheated oven for about 25 minutes or until they are slightly charred.
- ➢ Bon appétit!

Nutrition Info: Per Serving: Calories: 115; Fat: 9.3g; Carbs: 6.9g; Protein: 5.6g

Snickers Pie

Servings: 16

Cooking Time: 0 Minute

Ingredients:

- ➢ For the Crust:
- ➢ 12 Medjool dates, pitted
- ➢ 1 cup dried coconut, unsweetened
- ➢ 5 tablespoons cocoa powder
- ➢ 1/2 teaspoon sea salt
- ➢ 1 teaspoon vanilla extract, unsweetened
- ➢ 1 cup almonds
- ➢ For the Caramel Layer:
- ➢ 10 Medjool dates, pitted, soaked for 10 minutes in warm water, drained
- ➢ 2 teaspoons vanilla extract, unsweetened
- ➢ 3 teaspoons coconut oil
- ➢ 3 tablespoons almond butter, unsalted
- ➢ For the Peanut Butter Mousse:
- ➢ 3/4 cup peanut butter
- ➢ 2 tablespoons maple syrup
- ➢ 1/2 teaspoon vanilla extract, unsweetened
- ➢ 1/8 teaspoon sea salt
- ➢ 28 ounces coconut milk, chilled

Directions:

➢ Prepare the crust, and for this, place all its ingredients in a food processor and pulse for 3 to 5 minutes until the thick paste comes together.

➢ Take a baking pan, line it with parchment paper, place crust mixture in it and spread and press the mixture evenly in the bottom, and freeze until required.

➢ Prepare the caramel layer, and for this, place all its ingredients in a food processor and pulse for 2 minutes until smooth.

➢ Pour the caramel on top of the prepared crust, smooth the top and freeze for 30 minutes until set.

➢ Prepare the mousse and for this, separate coconut milk and its solid, then add solid from coconut milk into a food processor, add remaining ingredients and then pulse for 1 minute until smooth.

➢ Top prepared mousse over caramel layer, and then freeze for 3 hours until set.

➢ Serve straight away.

Nutrition Info: Calories: 456 Cal ;Fat: 33 g :Carbs: 37 g ;Protein: 8.3 g ;Fiber: 5 g

Coconut Cacao Bites

Servings: 20

Cooking Time: 0 Minute

Ingredients:

- ➢ 1 1/2 cups almond flour; 3 dates, pitted
- ➢ 1 1/2 cups shredded coconut, unsweetened
- ➢ 1/4 teaspoons ground cinnamon
- ➢ 2 Tablespoons flaxseed meal
- ➢ 1/16 teaspoon sea salt
- ➢ 2 Tablespoons vanilla protein powder
- ➢ 1/4 cup cacao powder
- ➢ 3 Tablespoons hemp seeds
- ➢ 1/3 cup tahini
- ➢ 4 Tablespoons coconut butter, melted

Directions:

- ➢ Place all the ingredients in a food processor and pulse for 5 minutes until the thick paste comes together.
- ➢ Drop the mixture in the form of balls on a baking sheet lined with parchment sheet, tablespoons per ball and then freeze for 1 hour until firm to touch.

Nutrition Info: Calories: 120 Cal ;Fat: 4.5 g ; Carbs: 15 g ;Protein: 4 g ;Fiber: 2 g

Raspberries & Cream Ice Cream

Servings: 4

Cooking Time: 0 Minutes

Ingredients:

- ➢ 2 Cups Raspberries
- ➢ 8 Oz. Coconut Cream
- ➢ 2 Tbsps. Coconut Flour
- ➢ 1 Tsp Maple Syrup
- ➢ 4-8 Raspberries For Filling

Directions:

- ➢ Mix all ingredients in food processor and blend until well combined.
- ➢ Spoon mixture into silicone mold and with raspberries and freeze for about 4 hours.
- ➢ Remove balls from freezer and pop them out of the molds.
- ➢ Serve immediately and enjoy!

Nutrition Info: Protein: 5% 12 kcal Fat: 69% 170 kcal Carbohydrates: 26% 63 kcal

Vanilla Cinnamon Pudding

Servings: 4

Cooking Time: 25 Minutes

Ingredients:

- ➢ 1 cup basmati rice, rinsed
- ➢ 1 cup water
- ➢ 3 cups almond milk
- ➢ 12 dates, pitted
- ➢ 1 teaspoon vanilla paste
- ➢ 1 teaspoon ground cinnamon

Directions:

- ➢ Add the rice, water and ½ cups of milk to a saucepan. Cover the saucepan and bring the mixture to a boil.
- ➢ Turn the heat to low; let it simmer for another 10 minutes until all the liquid is absorbed.
- ➢ Then, add in the remaining ingredients and stir to combine. Let it simmer for 10 minutes more or until the pudding has thickened. Bon appétit!

Nutrition Info: Per Serving: Calories: 332; Fat: 4.4g; Carbs: 64g; Protein: 9.9g

.

Cucumber Rounds With Hummus

Servings: 6

Cooking Time: 10 Minutes

Ingredients:

- ➢ 1 cup hummus, preferably homemade
- ➢ 2 large tomatoes, diced
- ➢ 1/2 teaspoon red pepper flakes
- ➢ Sea salt and ground black pepper, to taste
- ➢ 2 English cucumbers, sliced into rounds

Directions:

- ➢ Divide the hummus dip between the cucumber rounds.
- ➢ Top them with tomatoes; sprinkle red pepper flakes, salt and black pepper over each cucumber.
- ➢ Serve well chilled and enjoy!

Nutrition Info: Per Serving: Calories: 88; Fat: 3.6g; Carbs: 11.3g; Protein: 2.6g

Double Chocolate Brownies

Servings: 9

Cooking Time: 25 Minutes

Ingredients:

- ➢ 1/2 cup vegan butter, melted
- ➢ 2 tablespoons applesauce
- ➢ 1/2 cup all-purpose flour
- ➢ 1/2 cup almond flour
- ➢ 1 teaspoon baking powder
- ➢ 2/3 cup brown sugar
- ➢ 1/2 teaspoon vanilla extract
- ➢ 1/3 cup cocoa powder
- ➢ A pinch of sea salt
- ➢ A pinch of freshly grated nutmeg
- ➢ 1/4 cup chocolate chips

Directions:

- ➢ Start by preheating your oven to 350 degrees F.
- ➢ In a mixing bowl, whisk the butter and applesauce until well combined. Then, stir in the remaining ingredients, whisking continuously to combine well.
- ➢ Pour the batter into a lightly oiled baking pan. Bake in the preheated oven for about 25 minutes

or until a tester inserted in the middle comes out clean.

➢ Bon appétit!

Nutrition Info: Per Serving: Calories: 237; Fat: 14.4g; Carbs: 26.5g; Protein: 2.8g

Caramel Brownie Slice

Servings: 16

Cooking Time: 0 Minute

Ingredients:

- ➤ For the Base:
- ➤ ¼ cup dried figs
- ➤ 1 cup dried dates
- ➤ ½ cup cacao powder
- ➤ ½ cup pecans
- ➤ ½ cup walnuts
- ➤ For the Caramel Layer:
- ➤ ¼ teaspoons sea salt
- ➤ 2 cups dried dates, soaked in water for 1 hour
- ➤ 3 Tablespoons coconut oil
- ➤ 5 Tablespoons water
- ➤ For the Chocolate Topping:
- ➤ 1/3 cup agave nectar
- ➤ ½ cup cacao powder
- ➤ ¼ cup of coconut oil

Directions:

- ➤ Prepare the base, and for this, place all its ingredients in a food processor and pulse for 3 to 5 minutes until the thick paste comes together.

➢ Take an 8 by 8 inches baking dish, grease it with oil, place base mixture in it and spread and press the mixture evenly in the bottom, and freeze until required.

➢ Prepare the caramel layer, and for this, place all its ingredients in a food processor and pulse for 2 minutes until smooth.

➢ Pour the caramel into the prepared baking dish, smooth the top and freeze for 20 minutes.

➢ Then prepare the topping and for this, place all its ingredients in a food processor, and pulse for 1 minute until combined.

➢ Gently spread the chocolate mixture over the caramel layer and then freeze for 3 hours until set.

➢ Serve straight away.

Nutrition Info: Calories: 128 Cal ;Fat: 12 g :Carbs: 16 g ;Protein: 2 g ;Fiber: 3 g

Nori Snack Rolls

Servings: 4

Cooking Time: 10 Minutes

Ingredients:

- ➢ 2 tablespoons almond, cashew, peanut, or others nut butter
- ➢ 2 tablespoons tamari, or soy sauce
- ➢ 4 standard nori sheets
- ➢ 1 mushroom, sliced
- ➢ 1 tablespoon pickled ginger
- ➢ ½ cup grated carrots

Directions:

- ➢ Preparing the Ingredients.
- ➢ Preheat the oven to 350°F.
- ➢ Mix together the nut butter and tamari until smooth and very thick. Lay out a nori sheet, rough side up, the long way.
- ➢ Spread a thin line of the tamari mixture on the far end of the nori sheet, from side to side. Lay the mushroom slices, ginger, and carrots in a line at the other end (the end closest to you).

➤ Fold the vegetables inside the nori, rolling toward the tahini mixture, which will seal the roll. Repeat to make 4 rolls.

➤ Put on a baking sheet and bake for 8 to 10 minutes, or until the rolls are slightly browned and crispy at the ends. Let the rolls cool for a few minutes, then slice each roll into 3 smaller pieces.

Nutrition Info: Calories: 79; Total fat: 5g; Carbs: 6g; Fiber: 2g; Protein: 4g

Mango And Banana Shake

Servings: 2

Cooking Time: 0 Minutes

Ingredients:

➢ 1 Banana, Sliced And Frozen

➢ 1 Cup Frozen Mango Chunks

➢ 1 Cup Almond Milk

➢ 1 Tbsp. Maple Syrup

➢ 1 Tsp Lime Juice

➢ 2-4 Raspberries For Topping

➢ Mango Slice For Topping

Directions:

➢ In blender, pulse banana, mango with milk, maple syrup, lime juice until smooth but still thick

➢ Add more liquid if needed.

➢ Pour shake into 2 bowls.

➢ Top with berries and mango slice.

1. Enjoy!

Nutrition Info: Protein: 5% 8 kcal Fat: 11% 18 kcal Carbohydrates: 85% 140 kcal

Coconut And Blueberries Ice Cream

Servings: 4

Cooking Time: 0 Minutes

Ingredients:

- 1/4 Cup Coconut Cream
- 1 Tbsp. Maple Syrup
- ¼ Cup Coconut Flour
- 1 Cup Blueberries
- ¼ Cup Blueberries For Topping

Directions:

- Put ingredients into food processor and mix well on high speed.
- Pour mixture in silicon molds and freeze in freezer for about 4 hours.
- Once balls are set remove from freezer.
- Top with berries.
- Serve cold and enjoy!

Nutrition Info: Protein: 3% 4 kcal Fat: 40% 60 kcal Carbohydrates: 57% 86 kcal

Peanut Butter

Servings: 12

Cooking Time: 0 Minutes

Ingredients:

- ➤ 1½ cups vegan chocolate chips, divided
- ➤ ½ cup peanut butter, almond or cashew butter, or sunflower seed butter
- ➤ ¼ cup packed brown sugar
- ➤ 2 tablespoons nondairy milk

Directions:

- ➤ Preparing the Ingredients.
- ➤ Line the cups of a muffin tin with paper liners or reusable silicone cups.
- ➤ In a small microwave-safe bowl, heat ¾ cup of the chocolate chips on high power for 1 minute. Stir. Continue heating in -second increments, stirring after each, until the chocolate is melted.
- ➤ Pour about 1½ teaspoons of melted chocolate into each prepared muffin cup. Set aside, and allow them to harden.
- ➤ In a small bowl, stir together the peanut butter, brown sugar, and milk until smooth. Scoop about 1½ teaspoons of the mixture on top of the

chocolate base in each cup. It's okay if the chocolate is not yet hardened.

➤ Finish and Serve

➤ Melt the remaining ¾ cup of chocolate chips using the directions in step 1. Pour another 1½ teaspoons of chocolate on top of the peanut butter in each cup, softly spreading it to cover. Let the cups sit until the chocolate hardens, about 15 minutes in the refrigerator or several hours on the counter. Leftovers will keep in the refrigerator for up to 2 weeks.

Nutrition Info: Per Serving: (1 cup) Calories 227; Protein: 4g; Total fat: 14g; Saturated fat: 6g; Carbohydrates: 22g; Fiber: 3g

Almond Butter, Oat And Protein Energy Balls

Servings: 4

Cooking Time: 3 Minutes

Ingredients:

- ➢ 1 cup rolled oats
- ➢ ½ cup honey
- ➢ 2 ½ scoops of vanilla protein powder
- ➢ 1 cup almond butter
- ➢ Chia seeds for rolling

Directions:

- ➢ Take a skillet pan, place it over medium heat, add butter and honey, stir and cook for 2 minutes until warm.
- ➢ Transfer the mixture into a bowl, stir in protein powder until mixed, and then stir in oatmeal until combined.
- ➢ Shape the mixture into balls, roll them into chia seeds, then arrange them on a cookie sheet and refrigerate for 1 hour until firm.
- ➢ Serve straight away

Nutrition Info: Calories: 200 Cal ;Fat: 10 g :Carbs: 21 g ;Protein: 7 g ;Fiber: 4 g

Lettuce Wraps With Hummus And Avocado

Servings: 6

Cooking Time: 10 Minutes

Ingredients:

- ➤ 1/2 cup hummus
- ➤ 1 tomato, chopped
- ➤ 1 carrot, shredded
- ➤ 1 medium avocado, pitted and diced
- ➤ 1 teaspoon white vinegar
- ➤ 1 teaspoon soy sauce
- ➤ 1 teaspoon agave syrup
- ➤ 1 tablespoon Sriracha sauce
- ➤ 1 teaspoon garlic, minced
- ➤ 1 teaspoon ginger, freshly grated
- ➤ Kosher salt and ground black pepper, to taste
- ➤ 1 head butter lettuce, separated into leaves

Directions:

- ➤ Thoroughly combine the hummus, tomato, carrot and avocado. Combine the white vinegar, soy sauce, agave syrup, Sriracha sauce, garlic, ginger, salt and black pepper.

➢ Divide the filling between lettuce leaves, roll them up and serve with sauce on the side.

➢ Bon appétit!

Nutrition Info: Per Serving: Calories: 115; Fat: 6.9g; Carbs: 11.6g; Protein: 2.6g

Baked Zucchini Chips

Servings: 7

Cooking Time: 1 Hour 30 Minutes

Ingredients:

- ➤ 1 pound zucchini, cut into 1/8-inch thick slices
- ➤ 2 tablespoons olive oil
- ➤ 1/2 teaspoon dried oregano
- ➤ 1/2 teaspoon dried basil
- ➤ 1/2 teaspoon red pepper flakes
- ➤ Sea salt and ground black pepper, to taste

Directions:

- ➤ Toss the zucchini with the remaining ingredients.
- ➤ Lay the zucchini slices in a single layer on a parchment-lined baking pan.
- ➤ Bake at 2 degrees F for about 90 minutes until crisp and golden. Zucchini chips will crisp up as it cools.
- ➤ Bon appétit!

Nutrition Info: Per Serving: Calories: 48; Fat: 4.2g; Carbs: 2g; Protein: 1.7g

Peppermint Oreos

Servings: 12

Cooking Time: 0 Minute

Ingredients:

- ➤ For the Cookies:
- ➤ 1 cup dates
- ➤ 2/3 cup brazil nuts
- ➤ 3 tablespoons carob powder
- ➤ 2/3 cup almonds
- ➤ 1/8 teaspoon sea salt
- ➤ 3 tablespoons water
- ➤ For the Crème:
- ➤ 2 tablespoons almond butter
- ➤ 1 cup coconut chips
- ➤ 2 tablespoons melted coconut oil
- ➤ 1 cup coconut shreds
- ➤ 3 drops of peppermint oil
- ➤ 1/2 teaspoon vanilla powder
- ➤ For the Dark Chocolate:
- ➤ 3/4 cup cacao powder
- ➤ 1/2 cup date paste
- ➤ 1/3 cup coconut oil, melted

Directions:

➢ Prepare the cookies, and for this, place all its ingredients in a food processor and pulse for 3 to 5 minutes until the dough comes together.

➢ Then place the dough between two parchment sheets, roll the dough, then cut out twenty-four cookies of the desired shape and freeze until solid.

➢ Prepare the crème, and for this, place all its ingredients in a food processor and pulse for 2 minutes until smooth.

➢ When cookies have harden, sandwich crème in between the cookies by placing dollops on top of a cookie and then pressing it with another cookie.

➢ Freeze the cookies for 30 minutes and in the meantime, prepare chocolate and for this, place all its ingredients in a bowl and whisk until combined.

➢ Dip frouncesen cookie sandwich into chocolate, at least two times, and then freeze for another 30 minutes until chocolate has hardened.

➢ Serve straight away.

Nutrition Info: Calories: 470 Cal ;Fat: 32 g :Carbs: 51 g ;Protein: 7 g ;Fiber: 12 g

Vanilla Halvah Fudge

Servings: 16

Cooking Time: 10 Minutes

Ingredients:

- ➢ 1/2 cup cocoa butter
- ➢ 1/2 cup tahini
- ➢ 8 dates, pitted
- ➢ 1/4 teaspoon ground cloves
- ➢ A pinch of grated nutmeg
- ➢ A pinch coarse salt
- ➢ 1 teaspoon vanilla extract

Directions:

- ➢ Line a square baking pan with parchment paper.
- ➢ Mix the ingredients until everything is well incorporated.
- ➢ Scrape the batter into the parchment-lined pan. Place in your freezer until ready to serve. Bon appétit!

Nutrition Info: Per Serving: Calories: 106; Fat: 9.8g; Carbs: 4.5g; Protein: 1.4g

Lightning Source UK Ltd.
Milton Keynes UK
UKHW020625210621
385893UK00013B/1316